Ventura County LOOKING BACK

A PHOTOGRAPHIC HISTORY OF VENTURA COUNTY: THE EARLY YEARS

Presented by:

VENTURA COUNTY
STAR

Acknowledgments

This book was created through the collaboration of the *Ventura County Star* and the Ventura County Museum of History & Art. Instrumental in its realization were the tireless efforts of Project Editor and *Star* Copy Editor Don Scott, local historian Richard Senate and *Star* Marketing Director Monica White. It would have been difficult to complete this project without the gracious help of *Star* Advertising Administrative Assistant Jane Alvarez. Special thanks to the Ventura County Museum of History & Art's Research Library for help in retrieving and identifying all the photographs used in this publication and allowing *The Star* to reprint these historical images of Ventura County so they can be shared again and again.

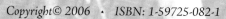

Copyright© 2006 · ISBN: 1-59725-082-1

Table of Contents

Ventura County Museum of History & Art

Clockwise, from top left: Chumash basket with lightning design; Lizzie Cornwell by John Nava; Amherst Pheasants by Jessie Arms Botke; Robert Gutierrez and his children enjoying museum's annual Day of the Dead Community Celebration; Camulos Harvest by Gail Pidduck; Lucrezia Borgia, George Stuart Historical Figure®, photo by Peter D'Aprix.

The Ventura County Museum of History & Art, an independent nonprofit founded in 1913, focuses upon Ventura County's art and history, both past and present.

The museum serves 65,000 people a year. Its unparalleled collection contains more than 26,000 works of art and historical artifacts from earliest Native Americans to the 21st century, while its Research Library archives over 150,000 documents and images. In addition to art and local history exhibits, the museum also displays the renowned collection of George Stuart Historical Figures®.

In 2007 the museum will break ground on an expansion which will double its size as a cultural hub for Ventura County's evolving communities.

The number accompanying each photographic image in this book corresponds with its catalogue number in the VCMHA Research Library Collection. The Research Library is a noncirculating, special collections library, open free to the public Tuesdays through Fridays, 10 a.m. to 5 p.m., and on Saturdays from 10 a.m. to 1 p.m. It is located in the Ventura County Museum of History & Art, 100 East Main Street, Ventura, CA 93001; www.venturamuseum.org; (805) 653-0323.

Foreword

Who among us has not daydreamed about what Ventura County must have been like 75, 100, 125 years ago? We wonder about the land and the people who lived in the county before the freeways, subdivisions and even the founding of some of our cities. We wonder who were the people who shaped the county, where did they live, how did they dress, interact and entertain themselves? Whether it is simple curiosity or a longing for something more, the past beckons us.

This book, like a family photo album, is intended to help us reconnect with our past. It is not a comprehensive history of Ventura County, but, just as a family photo album is random, sometimes incomplete and always full of surprises, so too is this delightful and informative glimpse into the past.

We owe a huge debt of gratitude to the Ventura County Museum of History & Art for opening up its Research Library and making the photos available. Also, special thanks to local historian Richard Senate, who provided invaluable expertise in helping to identify the people and areas that appear in many of the photos. He also wrote the introductions to the chapters. Project Editor Don Scott rounded out the process with his eye for detail and graceful editing.

We hope this book satisfies some of that wonder about the early days of Ventura County. More importantly, we hope this county photo album helps those seeking connections to the past to find them.

Joe Howry
Editor, *Ventura County Star*

Views

The lens of the photographer's camera is a portal for time travel. The images captured with talent and skill open the world of the past. It is a world far different from ours, with a slower pace, but one filled with promises. The vistas depicted here are of a Ventura County growing and prosperous. The dirt streets and towns show us a haunting world both remote and familiar.

Here, images of people look back at the viewer as they pause in their daily pursuits. Study their faces and in their expressions we see they are people like us, making their way in the world as best they can.

The views in this collection teem with life and movement, captured in an instant by the photographer. Here we see the moving wagons and ornate buildings. From time to time a familiar structure is seen – the old San Buenaventura Mission, the Ventura Odd Fellows Hall, the Port Hueneme Wharf. All give reference like a compass to where these pictures were taken so long ago.

Study these visions and think back to that time when things were simpler and the world moved to a slower beat. Reflect on those who came before and understand that, deep down, we are much like them.

Left: *Main Street, Ventura, looking west toward California Street, circa 1928. Note the new Hotel Ventura on the right and, on the other side of Main Street, the First National Bank building, where Erle Stanley Gardner had his offices as a local lawyer before becoming known as the author of the Perry Mason mystery books.* #20013

Right: *Overlooking view of the streets of Hueneme, 1895.* #4031

Above: Ventura from the surrounding hills, looking down Palm Street, circa 1877. Note the coastal steamer docked at Ventura Wharf. In the time before the coming of the railroad this was the best form of transportation to the outside world. #7785

Right: Port Hueneme, circa 1902. #3975

Below Main Street, Ventura, 1877. Note the wide streets built to turn a wagon around in the middle of a block. San Buenaventura Mission's bell tower is in the background. The dirt street would not be paved until 1908. #118

Above: *Santa Paula, 1904, looking toward South Mountain and the Santa Clara River. By 1879 Santa Paula was the second-largest town in Ventura County, with a population of 250. The city had its own post office and Wells Fargo station.* #7411

Left: *Main Street looking east, Ventura, circa 1890. Note San Buenaventura Mission at left (foreground), and the Anacapa Hotel one block down. The tower of the Rose Hotel also can be seen in the distance.* #35208

Above & Below: *Oxnard Plaza with pagoda and Oxnard Hotel.* #10662

Above: *San Buenaventura Mission, at the crossroads of Main and Palm streets. Note the four-room Hill Street School overlooking the community. Mr. F.S. Buckham was the first principal. The school was designed and built by William Dewey Hobson, an early builder, in 1873.* #1844

Above: *Looking west on Main Street, Santa Paula, circa 1905. Note the Odd Fellows town clock, built in 1905.* #7521

Right: *J.C. Hartman next to his team of horses on Ventura Boulevard in Camarillo, looking east toward the railroad, 1898. J.L. Sebastian Store at right. The small community of Camarillo grew up from Rancho Calleguas after the railroad came. The eucalyptus trees were planted by the Camarillo family.* #4165

Above: An Oxnard street scene decorated for a parade in the early 1900s. #4526

Right: Central Avenue, Fillmore, 1908. Fillmore was named for Southern Pacific Railroad official J.P. Fillmore. The town served as a stop between Saugus and Ventura. #9678

Below: Looking toward downtown Ventura, circa 1917. #5894

Above: Panoramic view of Ventura, 1910. #816

Left: A Chinese father watches his child take steps in front of San Buenaventura Mission at the site of Chinatown, perhaps celebrating the Chinese New Year. #28697

Above: Overlooking view of Ventura Boulevard in Camarillo, west of Somis Road, taken from the St. Mary Magdalen Chapel tower. #26122

Left: Looking across railroad tracks toward Fillmore, circa 1890. #3899

Below: Wagons and automobiles share Central Avenue in Fillmore, circa 1919. #9975

Above: An aerial view of Oxnard, looking northwest, before 1930. #26431

Education

Though there was an interest in education dating back to when Ventura County was part of Mexico, it wasn't until 1866 that the county's first grammar school was built. It was on Ventura Avenue near Harrison Street in Ventura. That same year, the Camarillo family donated its adobe on Main Street in Ventura for use as a high school. In 1871, the state passed a measure letting local districts sell bonds to build schools. Because of this, the four-room Hill Street School was constructed overlooking the community of Ventura. The brick school opened to great fanfare, with the high point being a song composed for the occasion and sung by the new students. It was appropriately titled "The Schoolhouse on the Hill."

Schools soon were popping up all over the county, and class

pictures began filling the files of historic photographic collections. These photos depict the styles and class sizes of the day. Frequently, older horses and mules were set to work delivering students to class. One charming photograph shows four grim-faced children making their way to school atop one donkey. Many times this was the last task for mounts before they were let out to pasture.

Education then was basic, with a focus on reading, writing, basic arithmetic and American history. Most classrooms were equipped with prints of George Washington and Abraham Lincoln, a map of the United States, and a flag. Most also came with a rack of hickory sticks, the thicker for misbehaving boys and lighter ones for errant girls.

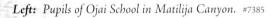

Left: Pupils of Ojai School in Matilija Canyon. #7385

Right: The first pupils of first Ventura School in front of the one-room schoolhouse at Ventura and Harrison streets, built in 1866. The first teacher was Miss Alice Brinkerhoff. The schoolhouse also served as a Congregational church on Sundays. #962

Above: Silas E. Coleman and his students on the front steps of Avenue School, Ventura, 1890. #2033

Left: The graduating class of 1894 from Kennard's Business College in Ventura. #3707

Opposite: Students of Montalvo School in front of the school, 1920. #3725

Above: Students fill the yard at Bardsdale School, later torn down in 1918. The school and community south of Fillmore were named for U.S. Senator Thomas Bard, from Ventura County. #8873

Right: Students take part in a lesson at The Thacher School near Ojai, still a prominent Ventura County school, circa 1900. #24

Above: *Ventura Avenue School girls pose for a photo during a milkmaid party.* #5355

Right: *Four Mill School pupils ride a donkey on Ventura Avenue, 1904.* #1915

Opposite: *Teachers and students in front of Somis School, 1895.* #1256

Transportation

From the days of the Spanish padres, transportation was important to link Ventura County to the rest of California. The slow oxcart gave way to the horse and mule-drawn wagon. Stagecoaches came in 1868, linking the towns of Southern California. With the building of Ventura's wharf in 1872, coastal steamers put in and landed goods, took away local products and served as transportation. In the early years, the wharves at Port Hueneme and Ventura were our windows to the world.

Better roads and bridges later improved conditions, but real strides in overland transportation had to wait until 1887 and the coming of the railroad. This opened new markets all over the world for Ventura County's prodigious yields of lima beans, beet sugar and oil.

After the turn of the 20th century, automobiles would replace horse-drawn carriages and stables would become garages. The car became dominant after the inexpensive Model T Ford came out in 1914. Automobiles came to rule the highways, bringing better roads, motor camps, and the freedom of travel to the common people.

These images are of a slower time, when the clip-clop of hooves and squeak of wheels were the sounds of transportation. Here, too, is the wooden causeway at the Rincon, which linked Ventura County and Santa Barbara. It stood until it was replaced by a proper road in 1924, the precursor to highways 1 and 101.

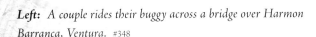

Left: *A couple rides their buggy across a bridge over Harmon Barranca, Ventura.* #348

Right: *Two gentlemen in a buggy in front of Ayers & Robinson Livery Feed Sale Stable, on Ventura's Main Street near the San Buenaventura Mission.* #3624

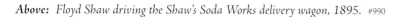

Above: *Floyd Shaw driving the Shaw's Soda Works delivery wagon, 1895.* #990

Right: *An early day bus transports a handful of passengers in Ventura, 1885.* #10033

Above: *Women stand in the field near a railroad grading camp, awaiting the arrival of Southern Pacific Railroad through Ventura, 1887.* #3871

Left: *Conductors and an early day train, passing through Ventura, 1887.* #3872

Left: Dr. Mott (first name unrecorded) gives an oration at the dedication of the Montalvo Bridge in 1898. #1439

Above: The Mercer brothers ride through town in a St. Louis automobile, 1903. Seated in the rear are Bert and Larry. Fred and Ed occupy the front seat. #5784

Below: A wagon and team of horses in front of the San Buenaventura train depot, 1890. #1025

Above: Dedication of the Montalvo Bridge across the Santa Clara River, 1898. #854

Below: Dr. Cephas L. Bard, his horse and buggy, with Mr. L.F. Eastin, editor of the Ventura Independent newspaper, and Senator Thomas R. Bard in front of the Rose Hotel, Ventura. #2312

Above: Ventura Auto Club, 1903. #5783

Left: Ed Mercer, left, and Sheriff E.G. McMartin (front seat), R.M. Haydin and W. McGlinchey (rear seat) in first county car, a Stevens-Duryea, 1912. McMartin and Oxnard Marshal William Kelly were killed August 20, 1921, by a murder suspect they had pursued to Owensmouth, a town in the western San Fernando Valley, now Canoga Park. #5786

Below: T.S. Clark drove his stage from Ventura to Ojai during the flood of 1914. He is pictured here in front of Dingman's Studio and John H. Reppy Real Estate & Insurance. #5263

Above: The Goodyear blimp Volunteer rests at Port Hueneme. #15858

Left: Automobiles line up in front of a garage on Central Avenue in Fillmore, circa 1916. #12385

Below: Couples enjoy the plank causeway near Rincon Point, opened November 1, 1912. The drive from Ventura to Santa Barbara took one and a half hours – a considerable savings from the seven hours it took by stagecoach. The wooden causeway was replaced by a two-lane road in 1924. #11356

Above: Joe Horner, seated behind a team of horses, rides an old stage and mail coach through Santa Susana Pass, between the Simi and San Fernando valleys. #15327

Above: Spectators gather in Fillmore on July 6, 1927, for dedication of a monorail. A Mr. P.S. Coombs proposed the novel idea, but it was never built and the money vanished – along with Mr. Coombs. #12392

Right: Local historian Charles Outland prepares for takeoff at Ventura airport, 1927. #9103

Below: A wagon and horse team in front of the Ventura County Power Co. Ware House No. 1. #8905

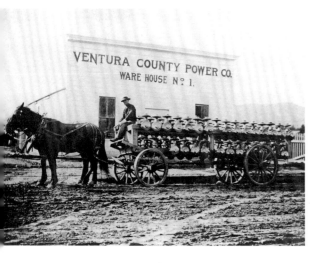

Above: The SS Pomona docked at Ventura Wharf around the turn of the 20th century. #871

Left: Allen White and a Union Oil Company truck, circa 1920. #27641

Right: The SS India at port, greeted by a large crowd. #13510

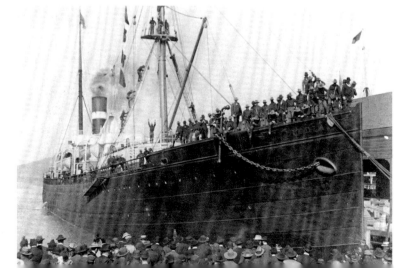

Above: Len Crothers and his "steppers" stand proudly near the top of California Street, Ventura. #3533

Right: Boys from The Thacher School, near Ojai, onboard a wagon in front of Ayers & Robinson Livery Feed Sale Stable in Ventura. #18774

Below: Mr. Phillips, driver for Samuel Cohn's delivery wagon, on Ventura Beach near the wharf. Note the lumber schooner tied up at the end of the wharf. #3118

Transportation

Above: *Old Hueneme Lighthouse, circa 1905. It was built in 1874 and moved by barge in 1940 to the new entrance of Port Hueneme Harbor.* #5269

Above: The first excursion train arrives in Ventura, 1887. Note Chinese railroad workers on the right digging the roadbed for the tracks. #12320

Left: Oxnard bicyclists, 1900. #5354

Below: An early collision involving a Los Angeles-New York Stage Company automobile draws the attention of onlookers on Ventura's Main Street. #14724

Industry

The roots of Ventura County industry can be found in its rich soil and mild climate. At first, ranching dominated, begun by the mission fathers and Latino rancheros. The native Chumash people became excellent vaqueros (cowboys). After flooding and drought in the 1860s, farming came to dominate Ventura County industry; in time it would become the lima bean capital of the nation. Citrus fruit also became a popular and profitable crop, with apricots and walnuts close behind. Production of sugar beets on the vast coastal plain would lead to building of the Oxnard brothers' beet sugar factory, one of the largest in the world at the time.

Later, oil took over, with strikes in the Upper Ojai Valley and Santa Paula. Full exploitation of the oil-rich Ventura River Valley became possible after the invention of powerful drill bits in the 1920s. That field became one of the richest in California at a time when the United States exported oil to the world.

Each industry attracted workers — men to build the bridges, railroads and wharves to bring in goods and ship out cattle, oil, oranges, lemons and lima beans. Over time, these workers settled here and joined the county's diverse population. Chinese who came to work in bean fields stayed to become businessmen. Mexican and Japanese workers, who came to take their places in the fields, later started their own businesses in a process that continues to this day.

These scenes show the dynamic growth of Ventura County with images of tilling the soil, grading the streets and tapping the black gold of oil from the land.

Left: Limoneira, a citrus growing and processing company in Santa Paula, alive with wagons, workers and teams of horses, circa 1915. #5917

Right: Smoke curls skyward from an outbuilding at the American Beet Sugar Co. factory in Oxnard. #9290

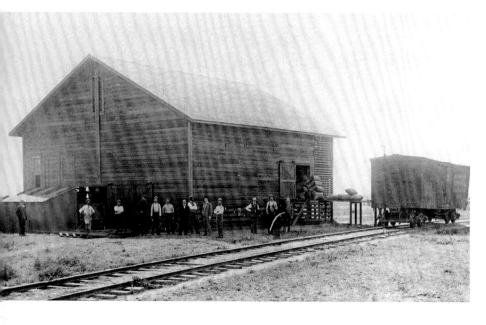

Above: Saticoy Walnut Growers Association's first car of walnuts, leaving for J. Bidderrident Co. #251

Right: A crew of engineers, led by Chief Engineer William Hood, surveying the Ventura coastline in the 1880s. #19202

Below: Workers at the William Dunn Drilling Co. in Piru. #15876

Industry

Left: *Ventura Oil Refinery, Bing Island, just east of the wharf, circa 1880.* #7442

Right: *A team of horses pulls the first load of asphalt from a mine in Devil's Canyon, summer of 1890. W.G. Wilde drives the wagon. C.J. Crothers and Bruce Mine, superintendents.* #824

Below: *Businessmen and farmers proudly display the first lot of granulated sugar produced by the American Beet Sugar Co. in Oxnard, August 22, 1899.* #3929

Above: *Men briefly halt their work at a Canet family apricot-drying camp along Ventura Avenue, near what is now Casitas Springs, in 1906.* #3914

Left: *Agricultural laborers in Simi Valley, circa 1895.* #1539

Right: *Lillian Dudley Bushnell picks flowers at Frank Dudley's estate in Ventura, 1904.* #18102

Left: *Mexican workers shovel gravel alongside a cement mixer at Casitas Dam, 1906.* #808

Right: *Workers gather oranges at McNab Orchard, Fillmore, 1896.* #11893

Above: *Blanchard Packinghouse, Palm Avenue, Santa Paula, 1910.* #2816

Right: *Hobson Brothers Meat Packing Co., Ventura, 1907.* #25316

Above: The gardens of Theodosia Burr Shepherd at Main and Chestnut streets, Ventura, were well-known for their exotic plants. Mrs. Shepherd's seed company and catalog helped to put Ventura on the map. Tower of Rose Hotel looms in the background. #3861

Right: Construction on Pacific Coast Highway, circa 1915. #30367

Below: Rotary rig at Standard Oil's Murphy-Coyote lease, north of Santa Paula, 1913. #8388

Above: *Ranch hands work sugar beet fields in Camarillo.* #32495

Left: *Two-masted schooner, the San Buenaventura, being built next to Ventura Wharf in the 1890s. It was built by James Daly and Owen Rodgers of Ventura to carry lumber from Washington and Oregon. The schooner was lost off the coastline of Astoria, Oregon, in the early 20th century.* #2302

Below: *Workers labor in an apricot-drying field, early 1900s.* #7327

Above: *Nathan W. Blanchard (standing at left), co-founder of Limoneira Ranch, watches a lemon-picking crew use 12 ladders to gather fruit at the ranch.* #5915

Above: Russell's borax mine in Ventura County's backcountry in the early 1900s. #2444

Right: A beekeeper carefully takes honey from a beehive. #3866

Below: First threshing outfit in Ventura County. #8579

Above: An overhead view of Medelssohn's Apiary near Ventura. #1890

Above: *Back side of Surdam's Dryer at Poli and Ash streets, Ventura.* #3910

Left: *Construction of the sea wall along Highway 1, Point Mugu.* #15790

Right: *Construction of Santa Susana Pass Road, 1917.* #9134

Left: *Two men push handtrucks loaded with sacks of sugar beets.* #9296

Below: *Workers make sacks for beets at the Oxnard beet sugar factory.* #9295

Above: *A ship awaits a load of grain on Hueneme Wharf.* #4064

Right: *Construction unfolds on the first Ventura River Bridge, west of Ventura, 1912.* #9209

Below: *Men supervise steam shovel operations on the Ventura County coastline, 1923.* #26944

Above: *The Ventura River Bridge under construction, November 24, 1912.* #9206

Left: *Frank Marr on a tractor on the Oxnard Plain, 1918.* #386

Below: *Grading California Street in Ventura, 1908.* #6134

Above: *Strathern Station railroad corrals, branding cattle, Simi Valley, circa 1915.* #5837

Above: Workers threshing lima beans, Oxnard, circa 1910. #2825

Right: East Indian workers harvesting beans on the Goodyear Ranch, Somis, 1910. Six thousand East Indians came to the West Coast in the early 20th century. Most eventually returned home. #8412

Below: Japanese citrus workers pause during harvest at the Teague-McKevett ranch near Santa Paula. #27999

Opposite: A group of workers at a typical apricot-pitting shed in the Moorpark area. #1417

Above: *Japanese workers arrange produce at the Limoneira packing shed in Santa Paula.* #8313

Left: *Two workers transport boxes of citrus fruits at Fillmore-Sespe packinghouse.* #8870

Below: *American Beet Sugar Co., founded in 1898 to process sugar beets. The town that sprouted around the factory was named for the company president, Henry Oxnard.* #3788

Above: *Preparation for sewer installation, Ash Street, from Poli Street, Ventura.* #6029

Left: *A Model T Ford, with a hay mower in tow, drives through a beet field.* #9115

Above: Derrick at work in Hueneme. #10615

Opposite: Ventura Avenue oil field, one of the most productive oil-producing regions in the West. Much of the development was done by Shell Oil Co. #193

Above: Two people seated on the front porch of the Ortega Adobe, West Main Street, Ventura. This was the birthplace of Ortega Chili Co., the first canning company in California. #4393

Left: Construction of St. Francis Dam, San Francisquito Canyon, circa 1925. The dam was designed by Los Angeles City Engineer William F. Mulholland. When it failed the night of March 12, 1928, it caused the second-worst disaster in California history. #26729

Commerce

Commerce began around the Mission Santa Buenaventura when small adobe shops opened to sell goods to ranchers coming to the church to pray. Like a magnet, the simple businesses drew more, all meeting the needs of the growing community. There were saloons that served the local cowboys and later ranchers. Hotels were built – fine, palatial structures like the Rose, the Anacapa in Ventura, the Hotel Oxnard in that community, and the Union Hotel in Newbury Park. Restaurants and shops lined the principal streets of every Ventura County community. These included doctors' and dentists' offices, and harness makers, dry goods and butcher shops. Hat shops were popular with the ladies in an era when going hatless was almost like going about without clothing.

Chinese laundries were popular as well as Chinese restaurants, such as Sing Kee's American Restaurant, where chop suey was on the menu. The old Ortega Adobe, birthplace of the Ortega Chili Co., became a popular Mexican restaurant in the early days of the 20th century.

Movie houses replaced the smaller theaters that had shown silent films featuring such notable actors as Charlie Chaplin, Mary Pickford and Rudolph Valentino, who visited Ventura County and made motion pictures here. In 1927, football hero Red Grange (also known as The Galloping Ghost) made a film in Ventura.

Left: Bustling businesses line Main Street, Ventura, circa 1928. Note Shipman Drug Co., at Main and California streets, and the Odd Fellows Hall, built in 1880, that stands today as one of Ventura's oldest buildings. #1086

Right: Foothills Hotel in Ojai, 1924. #4656

Right: *Wagon wheels collect outside of the shop of W.H. Harris on California Street, Ventura, circa 1884.* #3783

Below: *Citizens pose in front of the Signal newspaper office, Ed T. Hare Fire & Marine Insurance, a real estate office and a liquor store, on the south side of Figueroa Street, Ventura, 1877. Ed T. Hare put in the telephone service in Ventura with his nephew Win Hare in 1885. He connected local telephone lines to Los Angeles lines. In 10 years they had 71 subscribers.* #3028

Commerce

Above: *The Pierpont Inn, originally called The Wayside Inn, stood alone east of Ventura when first opened in 1910.* Glass plate negative collection

Left: *William E. Shepherd, Mr. Geberding, and others in front of A. Levy's office in Hueneme, 1890.* #4004

Right: *Santa Clara House, Main Street, Ventura, 1885. This is the present location of the Ventura County Museum of History & Art.* #1833

Left: The editor of the Ventura Independent newspaper, L.F. Eastin, right, stands outside the newspaper office, circa 1887. #5467

Right: Bankers attend the service counter at the Bank of Ventura, 1892. #1103

Above: Construction of the Bank of Ventura, 1891. #3535

Left: The Stagecoach Inn, also known as Union Hotel, Newbury Park, Conejo Valley. #1462

Right: Stagecoach Inn, Newbury Park, 1895. #5798

Above: Bartlett Bros. music store on the south side of Main Street, near Palm and Oak streets, Ventura, 1892. #30512

Left: Shoppers and businessmen pass in front of Santa Paula Hardware Co., 1900. Union Oil Co. of California occupied the second floor of this building. The building still stands as a museum on the corner of 10th and Main streets. #8883

Right: Wineman clothing store, 1895. Bartlett Bros. music store to the right. #3529

Above: Anacapa Hotel, built in the Ventura real estate boom of 1887, located on the northwest corner of Main and Palm streets, Ventura. The Anacapa Hotel was a rival of the Rose Hotel. #13226

Left: Interior of the Free Press office, Oak Street, Ventura, during the McKinley and Bryan presidential campaign. Ben Sykes, owner, is pictured second from left. Mr. Peak, at the counter, was the editor when this photo was taken in 1896. #3542

Opposite: People and bicycles pictured in front of A.H. Ebright Plumbing and O.T. Jones Bicycles & Supplies, 1899. During the era's bicycle craze, businesses such as this plumbing concern took advantage by subletting to bicycle businesses. #30505

Above: Swiss Grotto and Swiss Saloon on East Main Street, east of Valdez Alley, Ventura, circa 1890. #10196

Above: Gus Shepherd seated, William E. Shepherd on sidewalk, circa 1890. Fred Davidson on extreme right, in front of Gus Shepherd's Sign Shop; Phares Meyers, house painter; and Fred Davidson, carriage painter shop. #3537

Right: Interior of the Free Press office, Ventura, 1900. The Free Press was founded by local businessmen to compete with the rival Ventura Signal Newspaper. #3522

Below: Ross & Butler Hardware & Paints storefront in Santa Paula, 1900. #1402

Above: *Simi Hotel, built by the Simi Land and Water Co. in 1887 to promote development in the area. It was the terminus of a stage line that linked to San Fernando. The hotel was the start of what would later become Simi Valley.* #1850

Above: *The Ojai newspaper office, circa 1890.* #3972

Left: *Pioneer Meat Market in Piru. Pictured at far right is owner M.V. Clays, joined by George Miller at left.* #9003

Above: *The Bank of A. Levy, its founder at the window. Note the spittoons on the floor* #1407

Right: *Three men patronize the Santa Paula Saloon before Santa Paula voted to go dry. Note spittoons on floor. It was customary to throw a nickel into a spittoon if you used it any length of time. The tip was for the person who cleaned and polished the brass basins.* #9082

Below: *Fresh produce draws shoppers into Ventura Grocery.* #472

Above: *A. Ruiz liquor store, left, and the United States Restaurant.* #30448

Left: *Canned goods and household necessities fill the shelves at Clyde Stewart's grocery store.* #7154

Right: *Employees of a grocery store pause for a photo. Pictured left to right are Ben Fazio, Charles Guesuner, Ed Newby and Al DeLeon.* #5890

Above: *Will Wright, Andreas Dominguez and George Wilson in front of Saticoy Harness Shop, circa 1893.* #2607

Left: *Beronio and Lagomarsino, Saticoy, circa 1890.* #4058

Right: *Oak Street store, Ventura.* #267

Commerce

Left: *Wolff & Lehmann store, Hueneme.* #3982

Right: *George Anderson Shoe Store in Santa Paula. The store had previously been a harness shop.* #9058

Below: *Citizens gather in front of Owen Miller's Central Hotel in Fillmore.* #9965

Above: Rose Hotel, Ventura Courthouse and Theodosia B. Shepherd's seed garden, Ventura. #6138

Above: John Madison Co., seller of hardware, buggies, harnesses, and implements, in Saticoy. #5998

Right: Workers in front of James Fulkerson's General Blacksmith & Machine Shop, Somis. #8266

Above: *Phares Meyers Cigar & Paint Store, 1907.* #25312

Left: *Superior Restaurant, at 717 East Main Street in Ventura.* #5925

Below: *Several men gather outside Medley's Liquor Store, Main Street, Ventura, circa 1910.* #5923

Above: Servers tend the bar at Kaiser Restaurant, Ventura, 1907. #25310

Left: Interior of L.V. Bicycle shop, 1907. #25311

Below: Three men repair an automobile in the Reppy & Robinson garage, 1907. Note posted sign that reads, "All work in this shop must be done by garage employees." #25315

Left: Burdick's sign shop on Figueroa Street, Ventura, 1929. #14881

Right: Conejo Inn, Camarillo, circa 1912. #21473

Below: L.V. Lewis motorcycle shop, Main Street, Ventura, 1912. #4522

Above: *Ventura Chamber of Commerce caravan, 1915.* #5791

Left: *B & F Café in Moorpark, 1920.* #14676

Below: *The California Motion Pictures Corp. in Santa Paula, circa 1916. Silent films were made in Santa Paula starting in 1909 with the Gaston Melies Co. Two-reel westerns were cranked out here.* #1600

Left: *Firestone tire store at Main and Mill streets, Santa Paula.* #2812

Right: *Looking into the first garage in Ventura, circa 1916.* #1870

Below: *Coast Wholesale Grocery Co., Front Street, Ventura.* #26362

Left: *Visitors flock to the grand opening of Ventura Theater on Chestnut Street, August 1928. The evening performance included an organ solo, comedy, vaudeville acts, and the main feature, "Excess Baggage" starring William Haines. Tickets had sold out by 4 p.m.* #2501

Right: *Bill Milligan Sr. in front of Shell service station at Enterprise Street and Oxnard Boulevard, 1920.* #27670

Above: *Businessmen meet in front of Ventura Steam Laundry.* #6010

Left: *Automobiles outside Burson & Fowler's Mission Garage in Santa Paula.* #19059

Public Service

Ventura County public servants, from mission padres to local politicians, law enforcement officers and firefighters, gave stability for growth and industry. Good men always seemed to find the public eye in photographs, from ax-wielding firefighters to the escorts who greeted Presidents William McKinley and Theodore Roosevelt when they visited the county. Doctors who healed the sick and veterans of the nation's terrible Civil War were among the selfless people who gave their service to others. Numbered among them, too, are the elected officials whose dedication helped to build Ventura County. One photograph depicts a delegation visiting the battleship USS Texas, anchored off Ventura in 1919.

These pictures, despite their quaintness, should remind us of such individuals in our own time who come forth to defend the weak and battle fires. Public service always has been and remains a respected and integral part of Ventura County life.

Left: President Theodore Roosevelt's train arrives in Ventura, 1903. #865

Right: Firemen of the Oxnard Fire Department, March 2, 1913. #13462

Above: The Ventura County Courthouse, with the jail behind the building, circa 1880s. It had been remodeled and expanded from the original 1874 building. #9093

Right: The office and home of Dr. Fredric H. Huning, the county physician and surgeon, Santa Clara Street, Ventura, circa 1908. #33039

Below: Grand Army of the Republic, Union Civil War veterans, forms a line in front of Armory and Anacapa Hotel at Main and Palm streets, Ventura, circa 1898. #13512

Left: Ventura's first hospital, built on Meta Street. It was completed on August 1, 1887, at a cost of $5,492. Mrs. John Larmer was the first superintendent who maintained the hospital, and provided firewood and clothing for patients at just $4 per patient. The building was demolished in 1922. #522

Above: The original Ventura County Courthouse, built in 1874. #260

Right: Dental parlor of Dr. S.L. Stuart (in window) on California Street, Ventura. Dr. Stuart's dental office was on the second floor while his wife (in front) operated a millinery shop on the first floor. #3800

Below: Veterans of the Civil War, led by Major J.R. Haugh and Mr. E.P. Sandborn, march along Ventura's Main Street, circa 1890. #1112

Above: *Volunteer firemen gather at Egbert's Gardens & Driving Park, July 4, 1876.* #8903

Right: *President Benjamin Harrison addresses a crowd during his speaking tour through Ventura County, 1891.* #5387

Below: *The Grand Army of the Republic at the encampment at Plaza Park, Ventura, July 14, 1892.* #5337

Above: Supervisors and county officials at Ventura County Courthouse, 1900. #5326

Right: The Chinese Fire Company appears in a 4th of July parade, Ventura, 1874. The Chinese Fire Company was organized by Chinese restaurant owner and businessman Sing Kee. The crew would put out fires all over Ventura, beating the regular firefighters to the scene. They were cheered when they marched in parades and in 1890 the city of Ventura purchased a new fire hose for them. #364

Left: Company E, 7th Regiment, California National Guard, in Santa Paula, circa 1892. #4384

Below: President William McKinley and U.S. Senator Thomas Bard travel by wagon, 1901. Not long after his visit to Ventura County, McKinley was assassinated. #4437

Above: President William McKinley, seated behind a team of horses, rides through California and Main streets during his visit to Ventura in 1901. #8458

Left: Crowd gathered at Ventura Depot prepares a welcome reception for Senator Thomas Bard, February 14, 1900. #1304

Right: Elizabeth Bard Memorial Hospital, Poli Street, Ventura. The hospital was the brainchild of Dr. Cephas Bard, brother of Senator Thomas R. Bard, and named after their mother. It was built in 1902. Ironically, Dr. Cephas Bard was the first to die in his own hospital. #2335

Above: Carnegie Library, Oxnard. A gift from the Andrew Carnegie Foundation, it was built in 1906 for $16,000. It is restored and now serves as an art museum at the northeast corner of West Fifth and C streets in Oxnard. #7524

Right: Nordhoff Fire Department in action. #16056

Below: Oxnard Fire Department, July 4, 1898. #13461

Above: *First session of Superior Court in Ventura County's new courthouse. Judge Clark presiding, July 21, 1913.* #8397

Right: *President Theodore Roosevelt addresses an estimated 3,000 people at Plaza Park, Ventura in 1903. He spoke from the steps of Plaza School, which stood at Santa Clara and Ash streets.* #5749

Below: *Camarillo State Hospital, a mental treatment facility at the base of hills south of Camarillo, today is the campus of California State University, Channel Islands. The hospital also is known as "Hotel California," from the song by The Eagles, because of its drug rehabilitation facilities years ago.* #7726

Right: Women parade through the street, headed to the Ventura County Courthouse dedication, 1913. #12929

Below: Scaffolding surrounds Ventura County Courthouse during construction, 1912. Note the monks' faces on the ground, placed on the facade to remind visitors the city was founded by the Spanish missionaries in 1782. The courthouse was built in the popular Beaux-Arts style. Many locals complained of the cost, $250,000. #12593

Opposite: Fernando Antonio Tico (in hat), son of Rancho Ojai land grant recipient Fernando Tico, pets a horse at the dedication of Ventura County Courthouse, 1913. #12928

Above: Speeches and a rare electric light display marked the dedication of the Ventura County Courthouse (today's Ventura City Hall), January 1913. It served the county until 1962. #26056

Below: World War I veterans at Camp Lewis, September 6, 1917. #7178

Above: *Ventura Liberty Boys, enlistees for service in World War I, in front of Ventura County Courthouse, October 15, 1917.* #5276

Right: *First Volunteer Naval Militia of Ventura, prepared to fight in World War I, in front of Ventura Mill and Lumber Co., April 8, 1917.* #5257

Opposite: *Ventura Fire Department on the corner of California and Santa Clara streets, Ventura, 1916. It was built in 1908 for horse-drawn wagons. When the city modernized to motor fire engines in 1924, the Ventura Police Department moved into the second floor and the firemen were left with the first. It was an unhappy union.* #3548

Above: A number of leading Venturans mask themselves to avoid the flu epidemic, 1918. One out of every 10 Ventura County residents died from the epidemic. #263

Left: Chief of Police Earl Hume poses on his motorcycle with the Fillmore Fire Department, circa 1922. #8866

Below: Five men in front of a pair of fire engines at the Ventura Fire Department, May 1929. #12582

Above: A group of men, including several police officers, in front of Ventura County Courthouse with the largest haul of alcohol contraband on the Pacific Coast, 1925. The bust accounted for 65 drums containing 196-proof alcohol. Ventura went dry and closed its saloons, with the help of women voters, in 1913. Prohibition would last until 1933. The drums washed ashore from a ship off the coast. #1089

Right: A reception committee awaits Mayor Dimmick (first name unrecorded) aboard the battleship USS Texas, August 22, 1919. The warship was anchored off Ventura. The battlewagon served in both World Wars and is now a floating museum in Texas. #8284

Below: Highway Patrol officers pose next to their motorcycles in front of Ventura County Courthouse, 1930. #8519

Disaster

Ventura County has known its share of disasters, from the devastating floods of the 1860s that old-timers said changed the very shape of the mountains and destroyed the cattle industry to later shipwrecks and railroad accidents. But none was worse than a terrible night in March 1928 when the St. Francis Dam in northern Los Angeles County failed, sending a wall of water down the Santa Clara River Valley and out to sea. That tragedy took the lives of an estimated 400 people, making it the second most devastating disaster to strike in California history, in terms of lives lost, behind only the ruinous San Francisco earthquake and fire of 1906.

Photographs of the flood's aftermath reveal both the devastated landscape and the stark human tragedy of the event. These documentations of the disaster helped with insurance claims and in investigating what caused the dam to give way. The visions of utter destruction give only a hint of the magnitude of the flood and its horrific impact on local families. But, as in all tragedies, there were great accounts of heroism, such as of two motorcycle officers who raced before the wall of water to warn people and of switchboard operators who stayed at their posts to warn citizens with frantic calls. Ventura County would recover, but the scars left by this great flood can still be seen and felt.

Left: The SS Coos Bay ran aground at the foot of Palm Street, Ventura, 1911. The small ship was pulled off and repaired, only to crash into the Ventura Wharf in December 1914. Her cargo on that ill-fated day was Christmas toys. The hull of the ship is still buried under the sand by the Ventura Pier. #2061

Right: Cars at the Edison construction camp lined up after the St. Francis Dam flood cleanup, March 1928. Roughly 150 men were killed at this site. #8623

Above: *Damage from the Ventura River flood, 1914.* #1908

Above: *The world's first oil tanker, the W.L. Hardison, caught fire and burned at the Ventura Wharf in 1889. A crewman, wanting to know if the forward bunker was full of oil, had lowered a lighted kerosene lantern down the hatch, causing the total loss of the ship.* #3884

Right: *Men sift through rubble after an Ojai fire.* #8703

Below: *Southern Pacific Railroad's branch line to the Ojai Valley was washed out by the 1914 flood.* #1004

Disaster

Above: Men gather around a derailed train west of Fillmore after the 1911 flood. #10145

Right: Train wreck just west of Ventura, February 8, 1901. #485

Above: Workers attempt to restore a citrus orchard that was buried during the St. Francis Dam flood, March 1928. #18679

Left: Power plant, situated 1.5 miles below St. Francis Dam, before it was entirely washed away during St. Francis Dam flood. #18686

Below: Ruins of the St. Francis Dam after its failure at 11:57 p.m. on March 12, 1928, less than three years after its completion. Twelve billion gallons of water roared down the Santa Clara River Valley, taking an estimated 400 lives. #2877

Above: *Rincon Road washout after the storm of January 6, 1914.* #25908

Left: *A man shows damage done in an alfalfa field after the St. Francis Dam flood, March 1928.* #18746

Below: *Bardsdale Bridge, partially washed out by the St. Francis Dam flood, March 1928.* #10218

Above: Automobiles traverse a bridge on the Santa Clara River as people survey damage after the St. Francis Dam failure, March 1928. #2705

Left: Wreckage left behind from the St. Francis Dam flood, March 1928. #15382

Right: The flooded front yard of Isbell School, Santa Paula. #8616

Right: West end of Ventura Bridge, after heavy flooding. #18644

Below: An impassable mire left by the St. Francis Dam flood, March 1928. #18657

Above: *A man stands amid the wreckage of his home near Fourth Street in Santa Paula after the St. Francis Dam disaster, 1928.* #8611

Left: *Land that eroded during the flooding of the St. Francis Dam disaster is filled with silt from an orange grove, Santa Clara River Valley, March 1928.* #18742

Below: *A crane lifts debris from a citrus orchard after the St. Francis Dam flood, Santa Clara River Valley, March 13, 1928.* #18681

Community

Life in Ventura County's early days wasn't just work; it never has been. No look into the county's past would be accurate without images of the many clubs and other organizations that gave meaning to its people. Fraternal orders and social clubs provided service and support to the community. Here we see groups such as the Freemasons, Elks, Odd Fellows, and drama clubs that performed popular plays and sang the musical comedies of Gilbert and Sullivan.

There were bicycle clubs, part of a movement that swept the nation that found firm roots in the health-conscious people of Ventura County. Such organizations as the Boy Scouts and church groups provided leadership and education to the young as well as opportunities to meet friends and make a positive contribution to society.

Here are the movers and shakers of early county society. The civic and cultural leaders who led the way through innovation and creativity included men such as U.S. Sen. Thomas Bard; his selfless brother, Dr. Cephas Bard; and the writer Erle Stanley Gardner, who became known as the creator of Perry Mason. Here too are seen the contributions of determined women such as Theodosia Burr Shepherd, who began a seed company in her backyard, and Ester Cohen, who owned and operated a business long before that became the norm.

Left: *Ventura County Women's Club gathers for an afternoon picnic, circa 1920.* #12930

Right: *The first Boy Scout troop in Ventura, founded by the Reverend William Miedema, in uniform, 1921.* #18385

Above: Interior of the mission, circa 1880. Note the stained-glass windows before restoration. #13832

Below: Women's Relief Corps of Ventura, circa 1890. #5209

Above: San Buenaventura Mission, circa 1890. Note the wooden bell in the top element of the bell tower. The bell was last rung by President Theodore Roosevelt when he visited Ventura in 1903. #35317

Below: Members of the Flower Queen Cantata of Santa Paula Presbyterian Church, May 23, 1891. #830

Above: *Chumash Indian basket weavers on the steps of San Buenaventura Mission. Standing at right is Petra Pico. The seated woman is Apolonia Guzman and the little girl's name is Soraida Garcia.* #301. #830

Left: *A.B. (Pap) Smith, manager of the Bard-Perkins Ranch, with the Pleasant Valley Belles, 1890. Clockwise from the top: Clara (Willard) Hartwell, Peney Beesley, Lillie Hobart, Effie Lillie Olds, Jane (Pitts) Myers and Mary Johnson.* #5149

Below: *Traveling evangelists greet a crowd of young children at their gospel car.* #9062

Above: Ventura Bicycle Club, 1898. #3622

Right: A group of county women, among them Bess Arneill and Pansy Brewster, 1900. #25974

Below: Whist Club farce, 1898. Left to right: Edgar Norton, George Williams, Ed McGonigle and Jim Willoughby. #866

Community

Above: *Participants of the first Bicycle Club Run to Santa Barbara with their bikes, July 4, 1891.* #5372

Left: *A scene from a movie that was shot near Camarillo. The actors themselves (as opposed to stuntmen) performed this stunt.* #10125

Right: *Inez Farr teaches the wand drill, 1894.* #861

Above: *Automobile Club in front of Glen Tavern & Hotel, Santa Paula, 1911. This was the location of many important meetings.* #1393

Left: *Sixth annual district convention of the YMCA gathers in front of the Congregational Church in Ventura.* #15174

Right: *Members of the Oxnard Knights of Pythias, a fraternal organization founded in 1864, circa 1910.* #5252

Above: *The Adolfo Camarillo House. This magnificent home was built in 1895 and remodeled in the Victorian style in 1914. Don Adolfo was one of the most popular men in Ventura County. The home is now open as a museum.* #17883

Above: *Ventura County Calf Club, 1920.* #9117

Left: *The popularity of Douglas Fairbank's swashbuckler film, "The Black Pirate," caused everyone to want to be a pirate. Here, the Art Club holds a pirate party at the Bob Pfeiler Ranch in 1924.* #18380

Below: *The Breakfa-steers, June 1928.* #2492

Opposite: *Women pose in front of the Native Sons Grand Parlor, at the Native Sons and Native Daughters headquarters in Ventura, 1906.* #5748

Left: De le Riva family at the De la Riva Adobe, Foster Park. #15197

Left: The Ventura Lions Club gathers for a photo before departing for the National Lions Meet in Kentucky, 1929. #5234

Below: The Fife, Drum and Bugle Corps from the Ventura Sons and Daughters of American Legion in front of their tour bus, Main Street, Ventura, circa 1930. #8762

Above: *Berylewood, Hueneme, the home of Senator Thomas R. Bard, was built in 1912 in the popular Italianate style. Bard lived here until his death in 1915. His widow occupied the mansion until her death in 1937. Today it is the Officers Club for the Port Hueneme Naval Base.* #10474

Right: *Fernando Librado, Chumash Indian elder (center, seated), with E.R.D. Barker and Pat Forbes, circa 1913.* #10602

Below: *A wedding at the Faulkner House. Built in 1894, this Victorian landmark was designed by George Washington Faulkner himself. It stands as a landmark of the Santa Clara River Valley in Santa Paula.* #2717

Above: *Walter Scott Chaffee Sr., first mayor of Ventura in 1866, businessman and the founder of the Republican Party in Ventura.* #7506

Left: *Teodora Olivas, born Teodora Rafaela Lopez. Christened at Santa Barbara Mission on November 11, 1814, she died in Ventura on June 5, 1895. Wife of Raymundo, she gave birth to 21 children. She also oversaw construction of the Olivas Adobe in Ventura.* #12965

Community

Left: Angel G. Escandon, California assemblyman, saloon owner and mayor of Ventura, is said to have sponsored the bill at Sacramento that incorporated the City of Ventura and helped to form Ventura County out of Santa Barbara County. He is also said to have had the first billiard table in Ventura. #186

Right: Angel Escandon's wife. #3397

Above: Tiburcio Vasquez, California bandit who operated for 20 years, grew up in Ventura County working as a shepherd and a bellhop at Ventura's Mission Hotel before taking up a life of crime. He never robbed in Ventura County because of his friendship with Sheriff Pablo De La Guerra. #3072

Right: William E. Shepherd, Ventura, 1873. Shepherd was a crusading lawyer, newspaperman, advocate and leading Democrat in Ventura. #4431

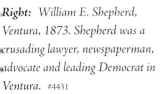

Above: Thomas R. Bard, the first and only U.S. senator from Ventura County. He, Wallace Hardison and Lyman Stewart founded the Union Oil Co. of California in Santa Paula in 1890. #11423

Left: Dr. Cephas L. Bard on horseback, Ventura, circa 1875 #222

Above: Mrs. Theodosia B. Shepherd, Ventura's primary grower of seeds. She was married to William Shepherd. An advocate of women's rights, she hired only women and was an early feminist. She died in September 1906. #5143

Left: Chinese businessman Soo Hoo Kow. When arrested by the city of Oxnard in 1911, he was defended by lawyer Erle Stanley Gardner in a classic case that went all the way to the California Supreme Court. #2356

Above: Erle Stanley Gardner came to Ventura County in 1910 and practiced law, first in Oxnard and then in Ventura. It was in Oxnard that he made a name for himself defending the Chinese. He would take up writing, first penning stories for pulp fiction magazines, then creating the crime-solving attorney Perry Mason. He would write more than 150 books in his life. #8674

Above: *Thomas Wallace Moore. His murder at his Sespe ranch on the night of March 29, 1877, was national news. The dispute was over land boundaries. In the investigation only one man was convicted of the crime, Frank A. Sprague. The crime is controversial to this day, a mystery unsolved.* #14631

Below: *Chumash Orchestra, first in Ventura County, at San Buenaventura Mission in the 1860s. Francisco Juan de Jesus Tumamite (Chumash Indian elder and early contractor), second from left.* #7346

Above: *Mary Pickford (right) and other stars of the movie "Ramona."* #9016

Above: *Mr. Achille Levy was born in Alsace, France, coming to Ventura County in 1874. He started a brokerage business in Port Hueneme encouraging local farmers to raise new crops. He paid for the seeds for the first sugar beets in the Oxnard area. This business evolved into the Bank of A. Levy Inc. in 1905.* #5569

Left: *Adolfo Camarillo, founder of the city of Camarillo, on horseback, Rancho Calleguas.* #17036

Below: *The Lopez Adobe was built above Ojai in 1830 by Rafael Lopez. The Lopez family owned the adobe and surrounding lands until 1925.* #5205

Recreation & Celebrations

Then, as now, the people of Ventura County knew how to have fun and when they did, they pulled out all the stops. The beaches were always a focus of fun, especially in summer months with clambakes and sing-alongs. The wharves and later piers have always been ideal for taking an afternoon stroll or baiting a hook to try one's luck fishing.

Bandstands in local parks offered concerts for local residents and passing troops. Once, famed march king John Philip Sousa played at Ventura's Plaza Park. In the era before radio, such concerts were important social events.

Sports also were a popular pastime, with communities and companies forming teams for baseball and football competitions.

County fairs continued the Latino traditions of horse races, fiestas and bullfights (in Ventura County, the bulls were never killed) that were held on San Miguel Day (Sept. 29). The first county fair was held in and around the new wharf in Ventura in 1872. The following year, it was held in Port Hueneme. It would then return to Ventura and become an annual tradition.

Parades also have long been an important part of Ventura County celebrations. Many holidays, from Independence Day to Fair Day, or merely the arrival of a passing circus were reason enough for a parade.

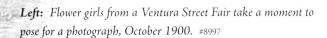

Left: *Flower girls from a Ventura Street Fair take a moment to pose for a photograph, October 1900.* #8997

Right: *An early panoramic view of the beach and pier at Hueneme.* #10589

Above: *A player lunges for the ball as spectators watch a heated match from the sidelines at the Ojai Tennis Tournament, cicra 1910.* #13507

Right: *Hueneme Grammar School baseball team in front of the Hueneme schoolhouse.* #19441

Below: *A hunting party in the Upper Ojai Valley takes a break, circa 1885. Note the Chinese camp cook at right.* #964

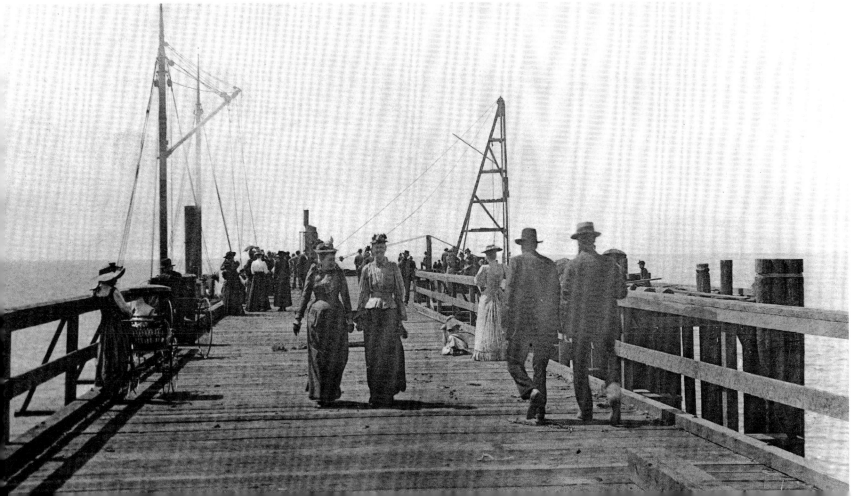

Above: *Bathers in the surf at Ventura Beach.* #1774

Left: *Strolling on the Ventura Wharf was a common pastime at the turn of the century. Note the pile driver and steam motor that strengthened the pier. Also note the little girl on her knees looking at the sea between boards of the pier as her mother watches with hands on her hips.* #9088

Above: Members of the Tuesday Club relax on a Sunday afternoon just east of the Ventura Wharf, circa 1910. #5461

Left: Beachgoers enjoy the afternoon sun and sand at Pierpont Beach. #12719

Right: The Pierpont Beach Pier at the end of Seaward Avenue, Ventura, sparked the Pierpont Swim Club. To join, one had to jump off the Ventura Wharf and swim to the Pierpont Pier. These dangerous adventures forced the city to hire its first lifeguard. The pier was washed out in the storm of 1932. At low tide, a few remains of the piles can be seen. #354

Above: *Beach visitors enjoy ocean waves near the Ventura Wharf, circa 1890.* #11348

Left: *Women enjoy a sunny afternoon on Oxnard Beach in the 1920s. Their swimsuits appear inspired by filmmaker Mack Sennett's bathing beauty films.* #26229

Opposite: *Rood's Orchestra, Fillmore.* #9951

Above: *Crowd gathers to honor Thomas R. Bard upon his election to the U.S. Senate in 1900, in front of the Rose Hotel at Main and Chestnut streets, Ventura. This view is looking south on Chestnut Street.* #4640

Left: *Proud fishermen display a catch of steelhead. Seated in the rear of the car is Fred Hartman and in front (behind the wheel) sits Louis Breer.* #5245

Opposite: *Young boys dress up as silent movie comedian Charlie Chaplin for a Charlie Chaplin Day contest held at Barns Theater in Fillmore. Such contests were held all over the nation – a testament to the popularity of Chaplin's "Little Tramp" character.* #10568

TONITE 7:15
BEBE DANIELS IN "THE MARCH HARE"
FOX COMEDY "HIS MEAL TICKET"

PEARSONS
BARBER SHOP

WATCHES

Above: *A young boy perches atop an extraordinarily large pumpkin at the Ventura Street Fair, Oak Street, 1900.* #508

Right: *Floyd P. Shaw, owner of Ventura's Acme Soda Works, exhibits his drinks for the Ventura Street Fair in 1902. Not shown is his famed Iron Brew, a beverage used in saloons as a chaser.* #780

Opposite: *A man looks to overtake his competitor at the harness races during the County Fair at Seaside Park in Ventura in the 1920s.* #1855

Below: *Lyons Hot Springs, in Ojai, and Ventura guests, 1892.* #3977

Right: Clowns and musicians at a Fourth of July celebration on Oak Street. #3592

Below: A large group, including Bartlett's Band, fills the hillside at Kenny Grove in Sespe, May Day picnic, 1878. #7753

Opposite: The Ventura Brass Band at Rose Hotel, circa 1885. #696

Above: The Ventura Bean Pagoda at the World's Fair in Chicago, Illinois, 1893. Ventura was the lima bean capital of the nation. Taxes on lima beans built the courthouse on Poli Street. #13321

Above: Traditional fiestas and horse racing marked San Miguel Day. These events included bullfights with matadors and the full pageantry of the corrida. In Ventura, the bulls were never killed and lived to fight another day. Here, spectators watch as a matador dodges a fiesty bull in the ring on San Miguel Day, September 29, 1873. #7337

Above: Charles Jones, Bert and Harry Mercer and others enjoy a bicycle outing, circa 1890. #50

Left: Several hunters return from a successful deer hunt in Frazier Mountain country, 1896. #9957

Opposite: White House Baseball Club of Ventura, 1889. #429

Above: Sespe baseball team, circa 1906. #11896

Left: Ventura County football team at the turn of the century. This team traveled to compete with teams throughout Southern California and beat the University of Southern California team in 1896. #5254

Below: Fillmore baseball team beside their tallyho and driver, which drove them to Moorpark and Camarillo for baseball games. #9683

Above: *The Ventura County Fair, held in Port Hueneme. A 10-mule team and wagon parade around the racetrack as fairgoers look on.* #9305

Right: *Fishermen cast their lines in the shallow waters of Matilija Canyon north of Ojai.* #2143

Below: *A party enjoys a picnic in the woods. John Carna holds a camera at the rear of the group.* #1259

Left: *The Boys Brigade of the Congregational Church gathers for a group photo, circa 1890.* #3860

Below: *Baseball fans gather to watch the Fats and Slims Baseball Game on July 4, 1904, at the Kensington Drive field in Fillmore.* #11894

Above: Santa Paula Union High School tennis team. #2804

Left: Boxer Sam McVey, from Waeler, Texas, came to Oxnard and worked at W.A. Roche's stable before entering the ring. His boxing record was 63 wins, 15 losses, 12 draws, 2 no decisions, and 46 knockouts. He was elected to the Boxing Hall of Fame in 1986. The photo was taken in 1912. #25541

Below: Oxnard baseball team in front of the pagoda, circa 1915. #25527

Recreation & Celebrations

Above: A crowd at Plaza Park in Ventura enjoys a visit from the Shriners Band of the Los Angeles Al Malaikah Temple. #8986

Left: Oxnard High School basketball team, 1926. #29079

Right: Charlie Hall, left, famed baseball pitcher of the early 20th century, was born in Ventura in 1855. When he was 18, he played for Cincinnati. He made his mark in 1906 when he played for the Boston Red Sox. He pitched in a 1912 World Series game that ended in an 11-inning, 6-6 tie. He played professional baseball for 27 years. He retired to Ventura and died in 1943 at the age of 58. #8693

Above: A scene from the 1915 movie "Ramona," starring Mary Pickford. The movie was based on the popular book written in 1884 by Helen Hunt Jackson about American mistreatment of Indians in Southern California. Mrs. Jackson used the Camulos Adobe in Piru (now California State Historical Landmark #553) as the model for her book. The film was also shot there. #1736

Left: Runners race toward the finish line at a Ventura High School track meet, circa 1900. #1444

Right: Fraternal Brotherhood Baseball Club, 1902. This team was Ventura County champion in 1902. #25484

Above: *A crowd gathers around Ventura's first football team, January 1, 1896.* #2029

Right: *Nordhoff and Ventura tennis teams pose for a photo, 1896.* #1675

Recreation & Celebrations

Above: *Ojai Valley Band, 1896.* #7155

Left: *Contestants line up along the starting line at a bicycle race in Santa Paula, July 17, 1897.* #388

Above: Los Angeles Chamber of Commerce at Ventura Street Fair, Oak and Main streets, October 1900. #570

Left: Ventura Fire Department rides a float in the Ventura Street Fair, 1900. #5030

Below: Dedication of the Women's Christian Temperance Union Fountain at the old Ventura City Hall at Main and California streets, Ventura Street Fair, October 1900. #575

Left: Crowd watches a "baby parade" through Ventura, Ventura Street Fair, October 1900. #25994

Right: Members of the Ventura Fire Department pull fire hose through town during the Ventura Street Fair, 1900. Left to right, A. Rodriguez, C. Baker, T. Crawford, V. Mungar, J. Mitchell, H. Johnson, J. Malone, G.W. Johnson, C. Kaiser (back of cart), H. Dela Guerra (behind wheel), and J. Behn. #5033

Below: The Ladies Executive Committee in a decorative wagon during the Ventura Street Fair, 1900. #3584

Left: *Ventura baseball team in 1902.* #5217

Above: *Ventura High School girls' basketball team, 1910.* #3650

Right: *Guests of Matilija Hot Springs, north of Ojai, in front of cottages, 1905.* #3981

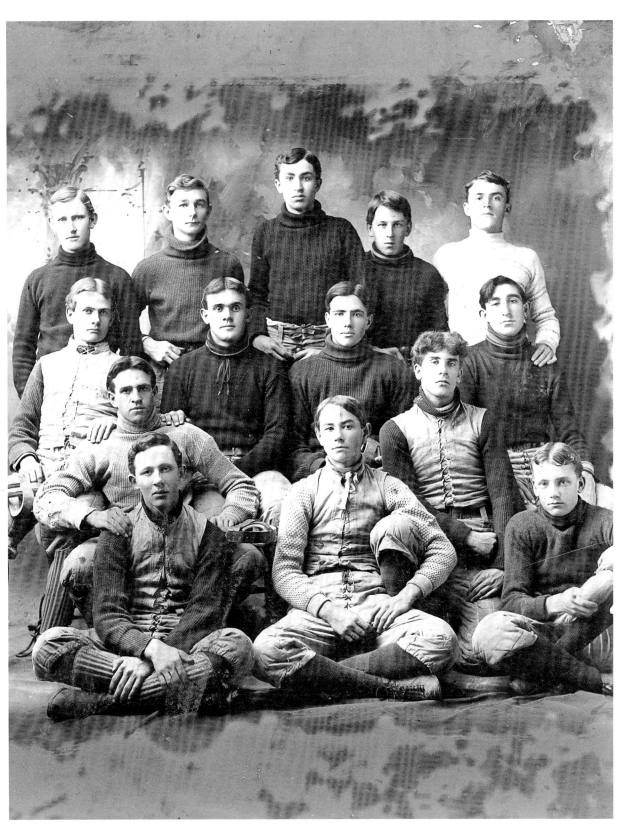

Above: *Saticoy baseball team, 1909.* #2590

Left: *Ventura High School football team, 1904.* #1108

Below: *Aftermath of the "Great Halloween Prank," November 1, 1908. When owners of the horse-drawn trolley in Ventura opposed the city's plan to pave Main Street (as it would cover their tracks), local citizens, dressed as Indians, broke into the trolley house and pushed the two trolleys into the beach and ocean. Main Street was paved a few weeks thereafter.* #3863

Right: The Fourth of July Boosters seated in patriotic automobiles gather on Oak and Main streets, Ventura, 1913. #3304

Below: Crowd surrounds the racetrack during the final day of the Ventura County Fair, October 26, 1920. #8583

Recreation & Celebrations

Above: *Ventura High School girls' basketball team, 1908.* #3651

Above: Men gather around for instruction at Jack Dempsey's boxing training camp, held at Soper's Ranch near Ojai, 1927. #10397

Opposite: Ventura High School relay team members, 1916-17. #19144

Above: Rancher and businessman R.G. Surdam and aides prepare to ride in a Fourth of July parade in Santa Paula. #3900

Left: Ventura Street Fair, 1900. Driving the wagon is Carl Fowler and seated behind him is the queen, Bertha Roth. To the left of the carriage stands D.W. Thompson and to the right is Albert Eaves. #1791

Right: Fritz Huntsinger spars with boxing champion Jack Dempsey at his Matilija Springs training camp. Mr. Huntsinger would become the leading oilman in the county, rising from mechanic to company president. He was a leading philanthropist in Ventura County. #25025

Above: *Golden State Dairy softball team, Oxnard, circa 1930.* #25526

Left: *Automobiles in front of Ventura Fire Department, decorated for a Fourth of July parade, circa 1920s.* #8271

Right: *Ted Henderson, the first paid lifeguard in Ventura, 1931. The Pierpont Swimming Club prompted his hiring.* #3396

Below: *Five men on a photo expedition, March 20, 1928. Pictured second from left is Deputy Sheriff Carl Wallace.* #2441

Index

Index

Index